THE SEED'S GATE

A Message to the Kingdom

Broderick R Barnes

Kingdom Khai, LLC

Copyright © 2021 Kingdom Khai, LLC

The Seed's Gate: A Message to the Kingdom, written by Broderick Barnes כבדיה and Published by Kingdom Khai, LLC.
www.KingdomKhai.com ©2021 Kingdom Khai, LLC

The Kingdom Khai Logo is a trademark ™ of Kingdom Khai, LLC.

All rights reserved.

This book or parts thereof may not be reproduced in any form, stored in any retrieval system, or transmitted in any form by any means—electronic, mechanical, photocopy, recording, or otherwise—without prior written permission of the publisher, except as provided by United States of America copyright law. For permission requests, write to the publisher, at kingdomkhai@gmail.com Address all emails as "Attention permission requests".

ACKNOWLEDGEMENTS

I'd like to give a special acknowledgement to The Hebrew Academy and Morah Minister Onleilove Chika Alston. It was in her ground-breaking course "Uncovering Hebrew Tribes of Africa" taught at the academy, where I was inspired to write this for class. Morah Alston is a phenomenal instructor and her many endeavors both in the US and Africa, have solidified her as one of today's leaders in uplifting the Kingdom of the Most High.

Thank you Morah for teaching the Kingdom.

Now if you will pay careful attention to what I say and keep my covenant, then you will be my own treasure from among all the peoples, for all the earth is mine; 6 and you will be a kingdom of cohanim for me, a nation set apart.' These are the words you are to speak to the people of Isra'el." (Complete Jewish Bible, Exo. 19:5–6)

A kingdom of cohanim or priest, a nation set apart for the Creator of the universe. In this passage the kingdom is am Yisrael, the people of Israel. The one who states this irrefutable fact is none other than the Creator Himself! So, there should be no issue when it comes to what our Heavenly Father said about His kingdom, that is not among those who say they abide by His word. Unfortunately, this is not true. How many people today claim to be in or a part of "the kingdom"? If we look at the two main people groups that claim their faith based on the "God of Israel", there are well over 2 billion people! (Judaism 101)

The problem is that these two people groups are religions. Christianity and Judaism respectfully, are not specifically identified as "the people of Israel". Instead they are known by their religious tittles. Is the kingdom a religion? What did the scripture say in Exodus 19? Is our Heavenly Father a liar?

"Heaven forbid! God would be true even if everyone were a liar! —

as the Tanakh says, Ro 3:4"

Despite what the masses in the world promote and accept as truth, the scriptures themselves say something different about the kingdom. The people group who are the citizens of the Kingdom are referred to by the King & Creator as Israel. He is not a liar, but why does it matter? Revelation 21 states the following, "Then I saw a new heaven and a new earth… Re 21:1, verse twelve, "It had a great, high wall with twelve gates; at the gates were twelve angels; and inscribed on the gates were the names of the twelve tribes of Isra'el. Re 21:1" According to the book of Revelation, when the Kingdom is fully restored there are only 12 gates in which one can enter in. Even for those who may oppose this scripture, saying that it's symbolism and not to be taken literally, the prophet Ezekiel adds a second witness to the matter.

" 'This is the territory you are to divide among the tribes of Isra'el. 22 You are to divide it by lot as an inheritance both to you and to the foreigners living among you who give birth to children living among you; for you they are to be no different from the native-born among the people of Isra'el—they are to have an inheritance with you among the tribes of Isra'el. 23 You are to give the foreigner an inheritance in the territory of the tribe with whom he is living,' says Adonai ELOHIM" (Eze 47:21–23). So, even if the physical entryway into the kingdom is only symbolically speaking about 12 gates, our Heavenly Father makes it plan and clear, even the foreigners to Israel are to choose one of the 12 tribes to live with, aka become a part of, in order to get the inheritance given by the King. Why does it matter who the actual offspring of Israel is? It matter's because of inheritance.

Merriam Webster's dictionary defines inheritance as; "the act of inheriting property, the reception of genetic qualities by transmission from parent to offspring" (Dictionary).

Those who are to be in the kingdom, though they may call themselves something different, are supposed to become part of Israel. Even picking one of the 12 tribes to join directly to. There is no gate with a non-Israelite name mentioned in Revelation's account of the coming kingdom. The intent of presenting this information is not to offend anyone, group, or people. It is in fact, to help empower and liberate the very kingdom aforementioned.

Damascus Gate, Jerusalem, courtesy of Pixabay

This is a message, to "The Kingdom", for "the Kingdom"! If we don't know the authentic identity of the people of Israel, how can anyone be sure they're entering the right gate? Who are the people of Israel, the physical seed due the inheritance promised by our King? Before we answer this question, we want to ask some tough questions.

Tough Questions:

1) Why do vaccinations have such adverse effects on African Americans boys?

2) Why does the highest percent of Sabbath keeping people in the world, live in Africa?

3) Why are European Jews looking for the "ten Lost Tribes of Israel" finding so many in Africa and not among themselves?

4) Why is the decimation of Africa's Congolese people, regarded as worse than the holocaust?

These are some very tough questions, but the common theme, is what will help us in our quest to identify the kingdom. Africa. Africa is the key that will unlock the truth that has been hidden.

How can the Kingdom of Israel be identified by Africa? Simple, the capital of the kingdom is and has been in Africa. The notion that Israel is a part of the Middle East, was not always the case. Prior to the 1900's it was known as a part of North East Africa and even further back a part of the Near East or Ancient Near East. Here's a reference from World atlas.com.

The term "Middle East" originated from the same European perspective that described Eastern Asia as "the Far East." The origin of the term "Middle East" is considered to be in the British India Office during the 1850s... The area now designated as the Middle East was known as the Near East in medieval times. It is reputed as the cradle of civilization as it was home to some of the most ancient human developments. (Sawe) Here are some various maps displaying this connection. In fact, there was not a physical separation of land between Africa and the Sinai Peninsula until the Suez Canal was finished and officially opened on November 17, 1869. (Editors)

The Suez Canal is a man-made waterway connecting the Mediterranean Sea to the Indian Ocean via the Red Sea. It enables a more direct route for shipping between Europe and Asia, effectively allowing for passage from the North Atlantic to the Indian Ocean without having to circumnavigate the African continent…..The Suez Canal stretches 120 miles from Port Said on the Mediterranean Sea in Egypt southward to the city of Suez (located on the northern shores of the Gulf of Suez). The canal separates the bulk of Egypt from the Sinai Peninsula. (Editors)

Two points of interest from this information, 1) the modern acceptance of the location of Israel has been influenced by British & western perspectives and 2) man physically separated the connection between Africa and Israel. Despite man's physical actions both through misuse of terminology and detachment of the land, the proof cannot be hidden. Israel is a part of Africa's tectonic plate.

The African plate's Northernmost part ends in Northern Israel and runs along the Jordan River to the South. (Israel as Part). Israel is situated along the border between the African Tectonic Plate and the Arabian Tectonic Plate. (Israel)

To sum it all up, Israel, the capital of the Kingdom, is a part of Africa! Now, given all this information on the actuality of the location of Israel, we now must talk about what happened to the people. "Le 26:14–16 But if ye will not hearken unto Me, and will not do all these commandments, Le 26:14–16 …33 You I will disperse among the nations, and I will draw out the sword in pursuit after you; your land will be a desolation and your cities a wasteland. Le 26:33" Here in this passage our Heavenly Father gives one of many warnings to the people of Israel that if they do not listen to Him, then He will scatter them among the nations. " 'I also raised my hand and swore to them in the desert that I would scatter them among the nations and disperse them through the countries; 24 because they hadn't obeyed my rulings but had rejected my laws and profaned my shabbats, and their eyes had turned toward their fathers' idols" (Eze. 20:23–24). There are many ways that Israel was scattered throughout history due to their overall disobedience to our Father. Our focus is tracing them through the deeper regions of Africa. By identifying the descendants of the children of Israel in African Tribes, we identify those rightfully entitled to the inheritance Father has promised.

In order to obtain clear and concise understanding of what we're about to go over, we most first address two critical components that will be discussed. First the usage of the terms Jew, Jewish and Judaism and secondly the perception of "oral traditions". Starting at the core the word "Jew" stems from the Hebrew word Yehudi, which means one from the people of Yehudah or Judah. Yehudah means to praise, specifically to praise YAH, our Father (Blue Letter). It is the name of the 4th son of Jacob, the name for one of the 12 Tribes of Israel, the name of the Southern kingdom of Israel, and the name of many Israelites throughout scripture. Also, the terms Judea and Judean, simply refers to the area of land and those who inhabited the area of Yehudah/Judah. More interestingly to note, is that evidenced by Gesenius' Hebrew-Chaldee Lexicon, the term Yehudi, "after the carrying away of the ten tribes it applied to any Israelite" (Blue Letter), see Jeremiah 32:12. Furthermore Yehudim the plural of Yehudi, gives us the term "Jews and or Jewish people" which is the plural of the word "Jew". They are all associated. (Jews). Judaism, however, is defined as the monotheistic religion developed among the ancient Hebrews…in accordance with Scriptures and rabbinic traditions, Judaism is the…total way of life for the Jewish people. (Cohen) This is from Britanica.com.

From all this we must understand that when the terms "Jew, Jews or Jewish" are mentioned they are linked to the terms Israelite and or Hebrew by lineage. Abraham was a Hebrew; his grandson Jacob became Israel and his sons Israelites. Jacob/Israel's

4th son Judah (Yehudah) connects us to the "Jew, Jews & Jewish". The error occurs when the religious view of Judaism is added in with the organic origins. Remember, the Kingdom is not a religion, it is a culture, a way of life. The definition via Britanica.com, mixes the two together. Judaism is comprised of two words, Juda, and ism. Ism is a "distinctive doctrine, theory, or practice," according to etymonline.com. (Ism) "Listen, children, to a father's instruction; pay attention, in order to gain insight; for I am giving you good advice; so don't abandon my teaching", Pr 4:1-2. Father's doctrine is the Torah, a national constitution and should not be equated to a religion. From his book *Ancient Near Eastern Thought and the Old Testament:* Professor John Walton states the following: "There is no such word as "religion" in the languages of the ancient Near East." …"Life was religion and religion could not be compartmentalized within life" (Walton 2006).

Now that we've established the authentic link between the word "Jew" and the words Israelite and Hebrew, as well as highlighted the view to disconnect the religion of Judaism from the way of life Father prescribed, we go back to Africa. In the book *Empires of Medieval West Africa* by Professor David C. Conrad, the following is stated, "The savanna of sub-Saharan West Africa was first described in writing by Arab travelers and geographers, who called it the Bilad-al-Sudan, meaning "land of the blacks" (Sudan is the Arabic word for "black person") (Conrad). In *the Chamber's*

Encyclopedia: A Dictionary of Universal Knowledge, Vol.9, Sudan is spelled two ways; S-u-d-a-n the modern-day spelling and S-o-u-d-a-n which is the ancient spelling. (Chambers) So-udan is made up of two words and in English, the (y)udan half of the word translates to Jews. This is validated by the similarity to its Hebrew word of origin Yehudah/ Judah. If we add that to the Hebrew word so, Strong's #H5471, which means foreigner, so-(y)udan means "foreigners of Yehudah/Judah" (Hidden Hebrews). In other words, both history and linguistics agree that the Israelites from the tribe of Yehudah/Judah or later those recognized by the general term Yehudim/Judean, were black and thus we must look at the biblical "Jews" as black.

This should set the precedent on accessing our viewpoint on "oral traditions". Many may have an apprehension to the use or exploration of "oral traditions". This based off of "New Testament" verses like Mark 7:8 which are stated in opposition to "traditions of men" as well as the negative aspects of the Talmud, a collection of Rabbinical Judaism's Oral Torah. However, many keys to our liberation are hidden in plain sight. While many of the links that will help to reveal the identity of the natural offspring of the Kingdom have been destroyed or covered up, some have simply been demonized to keep us from looking deeper into them. Oral traditions are one such category. In her book *"Prophetic Whirlwind: Uncovering the Black Biblical Destiny"*, Onleilove

Chicka Alston states, "oral history is key when searching for the Lost Tribes of Israel in Africa because history is passed on orally just as we have a written Torah that started off as orally passed on stories, history and proverbs" (119). "YAH said to Moshe, "Speak to the cohanim, the sons of Aharon"…this is how Leviticus 21:1 starts off. Our Heavenly Father spoke to Moses and told him to speak to the priests. This passage of scripture is the 31st Torah Portion or section of the Torah entitled "Emor", the Hebrew word for speak. Countless times throughout the Torah, Father tells Moses to speak or tell the kingdom something. "Then, in the presence of ADONAI your God, you are to say, 'My ancestor was a nomad from Aram, Dt 26:5". As pointed out by Rabbi Akwetey Amaah in one of his teaching entitled *Who are the Guardians of our story*, this verse is the command for Israel to orally speak a summary of their heritage as a part of the process of presenting their first fruits in the Promised Land, aka the Kingdom! "In this act Hebrews were commanded to become a nation of story tellers", says Rabbi Akwetey. In addition to that, Deuteronomy 32:7 says; "Remember how the old days were; think of the years through all the ages. Ask your father—he will tell you; your leaders too—they will inform you" Dt 32:7. This not only solidifies that it is a part of Torah to have an oral torah, but that it is supposed to be passed down to the next generations of the Kingdom.

    This leads us to the scattering of the Kingdom. We've already established that Kingdom of Israel, in North East Africa, would be scattered because of countless rebellion against the King and His covenant with them. There are 8 major captivities of Israel & Judah, as well as numerous Hebrew migrations deeper into Africa documented (Alston 89-91). It is here where we begin to identify the descendants of the Kingdom. There are several keys we need to look for in our assessment (Alston 97-98). Oral accounts of history and migration, linguistic connection between tribal languages and the Hebrew language, preservation of scriptural practices and the answers to our four questions asked earlier, for the icing on the cake.

"Most tribes have migrated from somewhere else to where they live today" (Alston 119), for example the Kikuyu, a sub-tribe of the Bantu say that they migrated from Israel to east Africa and then within the continent (Alston 119). One theory states the Ibo Benei-Yisrael of Nigeria are descendants from the Levant before and after the Assyrian and Babylonian conquest (Alston 128), while the Lemba have an oral history from Israel to Yemen and finally South Africa (Alston 170). The Erveh of Ghana say they're from the interior of West Africa, which ancient maps identify as the place where most of the enslaved Africans came from. This oral tradition says that they're "the warriors of Songhai in the Sudan" (Alston 145), or the so-(y)udan. But perhaps the Bassa of Cameroon have the most amazing migration story. Their oral tradition says that "they immigrated from Egypt thousands of years ago with their chief Melek, one of the grandsons of Judah, son of Jacob" (Alston 168). Melek was a military chief in the Egyptian army and didn't want to give up his privileges going on the journey with Moses. It wasn't until after the word of the defeat of the Egyptian army, did Melek fear revenge would be taken out on him and the other Hebrews who stayed behind. So, they fled south along the Nile then west across Nigeria until they ended up in Ngok Lituba (Alston 168).

Now how about we talk linguistics? First, we can quickly point out the connections in the very name of some tribes. Based on an article by Dierk Lange entitled *Origin of the Yoruba and "The Lost Tribes of Israel"* the Yoruba are believed to derive their name from the first Israelite King of the Northern Kingdom, Jerboam or Yarobam (Lange). Next, we have the Ga-Dangme of Ghana, who get their name from the 5th and 7th sons of Jacob Gad and Dan. This is attested to by Rabbi Akwetey of the Ga-Dangme in his video *How Important is Studying* Ones Origins. (Amaah). We then have the connection between the Ewe/Eveh/Erverh (eh-way) which is another way to say Ivri, or Hebrew in Hebrew (Alston 103). The similarity doesn't stop there, the Ewe/Eveh/Erverh language is also known as the holy language, this is based off its definition. Ewe/Eveh/Erverh means "child of Yehveh", a form of our Creator's name. So, the plural forum of Ewe/Eveh/Erverh means "children of Yehveh". Throughout scripture Father refers to Israel as His children. (Alston 146) Also, In Ghanaian the name Abena which can mean "preserves in spite of", is all but identical to the Hebrew name Abeneas which can be associated with "miracle maker". (Alston 143-144) Finally, the Ibo of Nigeria also have almost identical words in their language as in Hebrew. Including Abia compared to the Hebrew Abiyah "my Father is he who lives", amah compared to ammah "meaning mother or loved one" and atai meaning "real".

As exciting as any of these points are, they're just parts to a bigger puzzle. In order to truly solidify the connection, one must have a good understanding of scriptural practices. Specifically, the things prescribed in the book of Leviticus. In Hebrew "Vayikra", the book of Leviticus means" and he called". The overall theme of the book of Leviticus is that our father called The Kingdom to be holy, consisting of how to approach a holy Elohim and how to be a holy nation, a Kingdom. Wouldn't it go a long way in helping us identify the children of Israel by those who have preserved many of these practices? Well, every one of the tribes mentioned has preserved some of these practices. The Yoruba have preserved Hebraic wedding customs (Alston 134), the Ga-Dangme, Ewe, Bassa, Bantu and Lemba keep Sabbath and some form of circumcision, the Lemba and Ibo both have some sort of throne, the Ibo's symbolic of David's, the Lemba's symbolic of the ark of the covenant. The Ga-Dangme, the Ibo, and Ewe perform some sort sacrifices (Alston 114, 116, 117,119, 133, 134,147 ,148, 149, 169, 171). The most telling fact of all this is that it's their culture, their way of life. "Imagine a community of people who have never had a Sefer Torah but no tour by heart, who don't know the word kosher but keep kosher, who until recently didn't know they were Jews but live a thoroughly Jewish lifestyle", Michael V Gershowitz, Kulanu article. (Alston 150). In this article a modern Jewish writer finds it amazing that African's in Ghana are doing what he knows as a taught religion without being taught the religion. I hope we're getting the point.

Enter in these so-called "African American". Having identified so many descendants of the children of Israel all throughout Africa, it should be fairly easy to deduce how the African Americans are connected to the descendants of the children of Israel. African Americans or "blacks" were taken as slaves in the trans-Saharan and transatlantic slave trades from all over Africa. Including the places where many of these Hebrew African tribes were and still are today (Alston 193). If you examine the Slave Coast in Africa where many of the slaves were taken, we find countless Hebraic tribes such as the Ewe (Alston 193). To put it in perspective many coastal regions were known by their primary exports. For example, "the Gold Coast" was known for gold, "the

Ivory Coast" for ivory and so on. Well part of the west coast of Africa was known as the slave coast, because millions of African slaves were prime coastal exports (Alston 193).

Here's the connection, if the African Americans are descendants of the children of Israel like the African tribes, then we should be able to identify evidence of our ancestry as well. Now, these identifiers won't be the same as those who had their oral traditions passed down to them because our oral traditions were cut from us, but our father said even in captivity we will remember or come to ourselves.

30 For I know that they will not obey me, for they are a stiff-necked people. But in the land of their exile they will come to themselves (*The Holy Bible:* Bar 2:30–31). In 2009, Voyages the transatlantic slave trade database was created, it's a list that traces the geographic origins of Africans transported in the transatlantic slave trade. By examining the database, one will find that there's numerous names ending in y-a-h, which is part of and the short form of our Creator's name. Further findings show that the origin of many of the slaves point to the Ibo, connecting African Americans to Hebrews in Africa.

This takes on even more weight when we think of the negro spiritual song "Kumbya". Wikipedia states, "Kum ba yah" ("Come by Here") is a spiritual song first recorded in the 1920s...The song was originally a simple appeal to God to come and help those in need (Kumbaya).

Six of the 16 lines in the song are as follows; "Kumbaya, my Lord, kumbaya" (mrtibbs6912). Amazingly this is a Hebrew phrase, "qum-ba-Yah" and can be translated with the ba being a short version the Aramaic "abba' meaning Father, making the phrase "arise Father Yah". However, upon further study the ba in qum ba Yah, can be linked to Strong's H935 - bow', the Hebrew word meaning go, go in com". (Blue Letter) In this case we can translate qum-ba-Yah to mean "rise-up come YAH".

In an article on blackhistoryinthebible.com, the following is revealed about the song; "it is believed to have originated with Southern Slaves", it was sang in Gullah, which is also a Hebrew word. Gullah means "basin, bowl, spring" and it was Gullah spoken by slaves that inhabited North Carolina, South Carolina, Georgia, and Florida. (Black History) The Gullah language is a mixture of languages, so the Hebrew word for bowl or basin is fitting, since those are typically used for mixing things together.

If we add to all this that hallelujah, perhaps the most spoken word in the spiritual or religious "African American" community, in its simplest form is the pictographic Hebrew phrase meaning "look towards" as in "look towards YAH" to guide us (Ancient), it should be overwhelming clear that even in our captivity we have inherently remembered our Hebrew origins and our Father's name even without our oral traditions.

"For I know that they will not obey me, for they are a stiff-necked people. But in the land of their exile they will come to themselves 31 and know that I am the Lord their God. I will give them a heart that obeys and ears that hear; 32 they will praise me in the land of their exile, (Kumbaya) and will remember my name (YAH)" (Bar 2:30–33).

Lastly, it's very fascinating to point out that the first established black church in America has deep ties with the Hebrew language. In 1775 in Savannah Georgia, black slaves built this church at night over the course of four years. This church hosts annual Passover communion service with its sister church and have done this since its inception. It's pew's, which were built hundreds of years ago are still in use today! On the ends of these pews ancient Hebrew cursive has been scratched into the wood. (Alston 195-196)

This form of Hebrew is Paleo Hebrew not modern Hebrew so how did these slaves know paleo Hebrew? Very few of the slave owners in Georgia were Jewish and even if they were, they would have spoken modern Hebrew, not paleo Hebrew. The Lost tribes of Israel who have fled into Africa would not have known modern Hebrew because they would not have lived in the middle East when it was conceived. (Alston 196) This should make it abundantly clear that many Africans and African Americans are indeed descendants of the children of Israel.

Now, to answer our Questions. Why do vaccinations have such adverse effects on African American boys? The horrific answer comes via Mike Adams- known as "the Health Ranger". He's a Scientist, Founder and Director of a Worldwide accredited science lab and editor of NaturalNews.com (Ministries). The following is based on a video he did entitled *The Science Agenda to Exterminate Blacks*. Adams said, that "there is a concerted, organized, long standing effort, to eliminate African Americans from the human Gene pool". He says when testing diseases through vaccines, blacks and Africans are targeted. It's been going on for years exampled by the Tuskegee Syphilis experiments in the 1930's and the illegal testing of trovan in Nigeria, in 1996. He states that "vaccines are made from aborted black fetuses" and injected into people, specifically blacks. He continues, certain vaccines also can cause spontaneous abortions, and in Africa the Beta BCG vaccine, causes the female body to destroy, eat away at her own fetus, if she gets pregnant (Ministries). This is another prophecy for disobedience Father told Israel.

27 " 'And if, for all this, you still will not listen to me, but go against me; 28 then I will go against you furiously, and I also

will chastise you yet seven times more for your sins. 29 You will eat the flesh of your own sons, you will eat the flesh of your own daughters (Le 26:27–30). Summarizing his emphasis, he states, there is a depopulation agenda for all, but African Americans are first (Ministries). Why is there a concerted organized long standard effort to eliminate African Americans and Africans? Maybe the answer to our next question can help us find out.

Why does the highest percent of Sabbath keeping people in the world live in Africa?

Our Father has preserved a remnant in Africa who have been allowed to orally pass down their heritage and therefore have remembered the fourth commandment. It is the sign that marks and shows who his people are.

12 ADONAI said to Moshe, 13 "Tell the people of Isra'el, 'You are to observe my Shabbats; for this is a sign between me and you through all your generations; so that you will know that I am ADONAI, who sets you apart for me (Ex 31:12–13).

There are 20 million Sabbath keepers in Africa, the most anywhere in the world (Alston 104). This is a sign to show us who His people are. But with knowing who we are, we need to know that there are those against us, craftily conspiring against your people, consulting together against those you treasure.

They say, "Come, let's wipe them out as a nation; let the name of Isra'el be remembered no more!" With one mind they plot their schemes; the covenant they have made is against you (Ps 83:4–6).

Why is the decimation of Africa's Congolese people regarded as worse than the Holocaust? The atrocity of the Holocaust is absolutely terrible there were 6 million Jews murdered. However, in the Congo alone, not all of Africa, King Leopold II of Belgium, under the heading of Christianity took over the entire country and made it his own personal slave plantation. King Leopold made over what would equal out to be a billion dollars today off Congolese slavery and devasted 70 to 90% of the entire population of the Congo. It's estimated that million between 4-10 million Congolese were murdered at the hands of King Leopold II, however some say as many as 15 million. He is known for chopping off the hands and feet of those who could not produce his quota or opposed his tactics and. (Biographics) Remarkably in the 1700's over 150 years before Leopold, prophetess named Kimpa Vita who not only believed in Messiah but preached that the Congolese were the descendants of the children of Israel (Whirlwind). Did king Leopold have a hidden agenda to stop the spread of the Kingdom in the Congo? It's said that in the 18th century Congolese religious art displayed Messiah as an African as a result of Kimpa Vita's preaching. If we go back to Mike Adams video, he states that Planned Parenthood founder Margaret Sanger, called African Americans human weeds in 1926. Adolf Hitler patterned the Nazi narrative of genocide in the Holocaust after her model of population control. Adams said, "that there is a holocaust going on today and it's against black African Americans". (Ministries)

There's an uncanny connection to the holocaust that happened to the European Jews and the catastrophes that happened to Africans and African Americans. What is a holocaust exactly? Holocaust as defined by etymoline.com means "sacrifice by fire, burnt offering," (Holocaust).

Why are European Jews looking for the Ten Lost Tribes of Israel finding so many in Africa? The European Jews are finding "the Lost Tribes" in Africa because that's where they are, with many well-preserved evidence of their heritage. Our father did not make a religion and though there will be many that are not of bloodline descent that will come into the house of Israel, all of those who come in are entitled to an inheritance through the bloodline of one of the 12 Tribes.

I pray that we've achieved our goal. That goal was to accurately identify a people, not a religious a group. This is because there's an inheritance that is directly associated with the seed it's promised too. There are many ways the powers that be are trying to stop us from getting our inheritance which is the kingdom.

None more devastating than stopping the seed. Currently we are divided and fractured, and a Kingdom divided cannot stand. The two sticks need to begin to come together, all of us from Africa to America and throughout the four corners of the world. Many of us in Africa have been allowed to maintain our culture parts but there's an overwhelming influence to convert to a religion, Judaism or other. I don't feel that this is consistent with the Most High and His spoken Word. Because of circumstance for some I realize conversion is a viable opportunity to acquire the provisions for health care and worship and other communal needs. For us in America we have not been passed down those oral traditions, yet we've had the opportunity to gain the knowledge of the modern world. We carry the testimony of our Messiah and have access to the understanding that the Kingdom needs to take our ancient principles and make the necessary updates to apply them to today's world. Speaking to the entire Kingdom, we need each other, in order to get our inheritance.

In Hebrew, the word nachalah means inheritance. It's spelled with the Hebrew letters, nun, chet, lamed, hey. It's three letter equivalent is Noach the same as the name Noah, the famed builder of the ark. His name means rest, as in A state of quiet and rest from burdens, work or enemy. (Ancient)

The two-letter cognate of the same word in pictographic

Hebrew is simply nun, chet, and caries the understanding to "continue outside", because the nun represents continuance, and the chet represents a wall that separates the inside from the outside. But as we look deeper, the pictograph nun which is a picture of a seed and chet which is a picture of a wall or gate, gives us an amazing revelation. Our inheritance is the state of our rest, freedom from our burdens and enemy and literally is a picture of the seed at the gate or the seed's gate. In the ancient world, kings, judges, and elders sat at the gate of the city. (Brand) Holman Illustrated Bible Dictionary (p. 306).

> Are we ready to get our inheritance and sit at the gates of the Kingdom?

Nicanor Gate, Replica of the 2nd Temple known as Herod's Temple

Works Cited

Alston, Onleilove Chicka. *Prophetic Whirlwind: Uncovering the Black Biblical Destiny*. The Voices Publishing, 2019.

Ancient Hebrew Lexicon of the Bible, www.ancient-hebrew.org/ahlb/.

Amaah, Akwetey. "Questions With Rabbi Basil - How Important Is Studying Ones Origins." *YouTube*, YouTube, 9 Mar. 2017, www.youtube.com/watch?v=tVAOyaT3P44.

Biographics. "Leopold II of Belgium: The Biggest Coverup In European History." *YouTube*, YouTube, 26 Sept. 2018, www.youtube.com/watch?v=dTq6Hnkpw2s.

Black History In The Bible "And because I tell you the truth. "Kumbaya (Kum-Ba-Yah): Did Black Slaves Sing Songs In Hebrew?" *Black History In The Bible*, 5 Aug. 2018, www.blackhistoryinthebible.com/the-evidence/kum-ba-yah-did-black-slaves-sing-songs-in-hebrew/.

Brand, Chad, et al. *Holman Illustrated Bible Dictionary*. Holman Reference, 2015.

Chambers Encyclopedia: a Dictionary of Universal Knowledge. Vol. 9, William & Robert Chambers, 1899.

Cohen, Gerson D., et al. "Judaism." *Encyclopædia Britannica*, Encyclopædia Britannica, Inc., 8 Feb. 2019, www.britannica.com/topic/Judaism.

Conrad, David C. *Empires of Medieval West Africa: Ghana, Mali, and Songhay*. Chelsea House Publishers, 2010.

"Dictionary by Merriam-Webster: America's Most-Trusted Online Dictionary." *Merriam-Webster*, Merriam-Webster, www.merriam-webster.com/.

Editors, History.com. "Suez Canal." *History.com*, A&E Television Networks, 16 Feb. 2018, www.history.com/topics/africa/suez-canal.

"Genesis 1:1 (KJV)." *Blue Letter Bible*, www.blueletterbible.org/lang/Lexicon/Lexicon.cfm?strongs=H3064&t=KJV.

"Hidden Hebrews 2 - Children of Judah." *YouTube*, 10 Dec. 2017, youtu.be/MzVqX01IUA0.

"Holocaust | Search Online Etymology Dictionary." *Index*, www.etymonline.com/search?q=holocaust.

"Ism | Search Online Etymology Dictionary." *Index*, www.etymonline.com/search?q=ism.

"Israel." *Encyclopedia of the Nations*, www.nationsencyclopedia.com/geography/Indonesia-to-Mongolia/Israel.html.

"Israel As Part of a Broader African Dynamic." *Israel Rising*, 16 Mar. 2016, israelrising.com/israel-part-broader-african-dynamic/.

"Jews." *Wikipedia*, Wikimedia Foundation, 3 June 2019, en.wikipedia.org/wiki/Jews.

Judaism 101: Jewish Population, www.jewfaq.org/populatn.htm https://www.learnreligions.com/christianity-statistics-700533.

"Kumbaya." *Wikipedia*, Wikimedia Foundation, 5 May 2019, en.wikipedia.org/wiki/Kumbaya.

Lange, Dierk. "Origin of the Yoruba and 'The Lost Tribes of Israel.'" *Http://Dierklange.com*, dierklange.com/.

Ministries, Teotw. "The Science Agenda to Exterminate Blacks." *YouTube*, YouTube, 7 Nov. 2017, www.youtube.com/watch?v=fHMlTL2VPl0&feature=youtu.be.

mrtibbs6912. "Kumbaya My Lord." *YouTube*, YouTube, 4 Nov. 2007, www.youtube.com/watch?v=vo9AH4vG2wA.

Sawe, Benjamin Elisha. "Why Is It Called the Middle East?" *WorldAtlas*, 25 Apr. 2017, www.worldatlas.com/articles/why-is-it-called-the-middle-east.html.

Walton, J H. "Ancient Near Eastern Thought and the Old Testament." *Amazon*, Amazon, 2006, www.amazon.com/Ancient-Near-Eastern-Thought-Testament/dp/1540960218.

Whirlwind, Prophetic. "#SayHerName Kimpa Vita The Congolese Prophetess Who Preached The Truth!" *YouTube*, YouTube, 27 Nov. 2018, www.youtube.com/watch?v=9ESgTw3obWo.

www.ingramcontent.com/pod-product-compliance
Lightning Source LLC
Chambersburg PA
CBHW041746040426
42444CB00004B/188